...Yeah and?

A 10-week look
at the basics of
Christianity and what
it actually means

SUZI STOCK

**kevin
mayhew**

First published in 2003 by

KEVIN MAYHEW LTD
Buxhall, Stowmarket, Suffolk, IP14 3BW
E-mail: info@kevinmayhewltd.com

KINGSGATE PUBLISHING INC
1000 Pannell Street, Suite G, Columbia, MO 65201
E-mail: sales@kingsgatepublishing.com

9 8 7 6 5 4 3 2 1 0

ISBN 1 84417 079 9
Catalogue No 1500593

Cover design by Jonathan Stroulger
Typesetting by Richard Weaver

Printed and bound in Great Britain

Contents

The 10 sessions will be about 40 minutes on average and will include a weekly speaker for 5 minutes on the topic with specific points to draw out, backed with scripture and including personal testimony. There will be group discussion/activities and prayer. The young people can follow the activities in the book, which will include questions/thoughts/facts/verses that they can look at in their own time – you need to ensure that you don't do too much in the sessions.

Acknowledgements

The author and publishers would like to thank the following for permission to reproduce copyright material.

Bucks Music Ltd for permission to reproduce the words to 'Message of the Cross' by Martin Smith (page 7), © Curious? Music UK/Administered in the UK by Bucks Music Ltd, Onward House, 11 Uxbridge Street, London W8 7TQ.

World Wide Message Tribe, for permission to reproduce the quiz on page 14, from *Get God 2000*, published by HarperCollins, and © 2000 The Message Trust, used by permission of The Message; and to adapt 'The ABC of Starting Over' on page 38.

Kingsway Communications for permission to reproduce the words to 'For the Cross' by Matt Redman and Beth Redman (page 17), © 1986 Thankyou Music, administered by worshiptogether.com songs, excluding UK and Europe, administered by Kingsway Music, tym@kingsway.co.uk.

Agape Ministries Ltd, Fairgate House, Kings Road, Tyseley, Birmingham B11 2AA, telephone 0121 765 4404, for permission to reproduce the illustration on page 24 from *Knowing God Personally*, © 2001 Agapé.

Every effort has been made to trace the owners of copyright material (particularly the text on page 43), and we hope that no copyright has been infringed. Pardon is sought and apology made if the contrary be the case, and a correction will be made in any reprint of this book.

Just a fashion accessory? (1)

Looking at the cross –
who Jesus was, what he did and why

Muffins and drinks

Icebreaker question in groups

On pieces of paper each write three things about yourself – two must be true and one must be a lie. Read them out for each person and guess which is the lie.

Explain/introduce course

Video clip

The Matrix (24min 25sec into film for 4min 24sec) – explanation and link to theme. The purpose of the course is to 'know what is really true, not what is nearly true'.

Testimony

From someone who is a Christian about how they came to accept and know the truth. Include a talk about the message of the cross – why and how Jesus died and what it means for us today.

Group time discussion questions

• Answer and discuss a few of these questions:
  – Why do people wear crosses? (see page 6)
  – Why should becoming a Christian change the way you live?
  – Would you die for any of your friends or family?
  – Would you die for your enemies?
  – Have you ever believed something was true and then found out it wasn't? (e.g. how to pronounce a name, or the stork didn't really exist, or the words of a song were different to what you thought, etc.)
  – How would you feel if you woke up this morning and were told your whole life was a dream?
• Read 'The Ragman' story (see page 8).

Prayer time in small groups and offer red jellybeans as a sign of accepting the truth.

Just a fashion accessory?

How many people do you know who wear a cross?
Ever seen someone wear a . . . little electric chair?

> The cross was one of the
> cruellest forms of execution
> known to man

So why do people wear crosses round their necks?

READ: 'The Ragman' story

Jesus died for the things we have done wrong and for the wrong things done to us. These are called 'sins'. Sin is about selfishness. It's spelt s-I-n. That's 'I' in the middle – when our life is all about us, we do what we want not what God wants. These things make us, and the world around us, unclean.

READ: Mark 7:1-23

This rubbish gets in the way of us and God, so because God loves us so much he did what he had to do and paid the price. He sent his Son – Jesus – to pay the price for us by dying on the cross.

READ: 1 Peter 2:24

> If you miss the mark by a metre
> or a mile, you still miss the mark
> (Romans 3:23)

We have all done stuff wrong and this separates us from God. He wants us to know him and to have a friendship with him so that's why Jesus had to die for us.

**That's why we wear a cross –
to remind us of what Jesus went through for us.**

So what?

Read through and discuss the words of this song...

MESSAGE OF THE CROSS
Martin Smith

*This is the message of the cross, that we can be free,
to live in the victory, and turn from our sin,
my precious Lord Jesus, with sinners you died,
for there you revealed your love and you laid down your life.
This is the message of the cross, that we can be free,
to lay all our burdens here, at the foot of the tree,
the cross was the shame of the world, but the glory of God,
for Jesus you conquered sin and you gave us new life!
You set me free when I came to the cross,
poured out your blood for I was broken and lost,
there I was healed and you covered my sin,
it's there you saved me, this is the message of the cross.
This is the message of the cross, that we can be free,
to hunger for heaven, to hunger for thee,
the cross is such foolishness to the perishing,
but to us who are being saved, it is the power of God!
You set us free when we come to the cross,
you pour out your blood for we are broken and lost,
here we are healed and you cover our sin,
it's here you save us,
this is the message of the cross . . .*

SO PRAY . . .

Thank God for what he has done for you through Jesus dying on the cross. Ask him to help you understand what it means for your life as you go through this course.

The Ragman

Even before the dawn one Friday morning I noticed a young man, handsome and strong, walking the alleys of our city. He was pulling an old cart filled with clothes both bright and new, and he was calling in a clear, tenor voice: 'Rags!'

Ah, the air was foul and the first light filthy to be crossed by such sweet music. 'Rags! New rags for old! I take your tired rags! Rags!'

'Now this is a wonder,' I thought to myself, for the man stood six-feet-four, and his arms were like tree limbs, hard and muscular, and his eyes flashed intelligence. Could he find no better job than this, to be a ragman in the inner city?

I followed him. My curiosity drove me. And I wasn't disappointed. Soon the ragman saw a woman sitting on her back porch. She was sobbing into a handkerchief, sighing, and shedding a thousand tears. Her knees and elbows made a sad X. Her shoulders shook. Her heart was breaking. The ragman stopped the cart. Quietly, he walked to the woman, stepping round tin cans, dead toys and 'Pampers'. 'Give me your rag,' he said so gently, 'and I'll give you another.' He slipped the handkerchief from her eyes. She looked up, and he laid across her palm a linen cloth so clean and new that it shone. She blinked from the gift to the giver.

Then, as he began to pull his cart again, the ragman did a strange thing; he put the stained handkerchief to his own face; and then he began to weep, to sob as grievously as she had done, his shoulders shaking. Yet she was left without a tear. 'This is a wonder,' I breathed to myself, and I followed the sobbing ragman like a child who cannot turn away from mystery. 'Rags! Rags! New rags for old!' In a little while, when the sky showed grey behind the rooftops and I could see the shredded curtains hanging out of black windows, the ragman came upon a little girl whose head was wrapped in a bandage. A single line of blood ran down her cheek. Now the tall ragman looked down on the child with pity, and he drew a lovely yellow bonnet from his cart. 'Give me your rag,' he said tracing his own line on her cheek, 'and I'll give you mine.' The child could only gaze at him while he loosened the bandage, removed it, and tied it to his own head. The bonnet he set on hers. And I gasped at what I saw, for with the bandage went the wound! Against his brow it ran a darker, more substantial blood – his own! 'Rags! Rags! I take old rags!' cried the sobbing, bleeding, strong, intelligent man. The sun hurt both the sky and my eyes now; the ragman seemed more and more to hurry.

'Are you going to work?' he asked a man who leaned up against a telephone pole. The man shook his head. The ragman pressed him: 'Do you have a job?'

'Are you crazy?' sneered the other. He pulled away from the pole, revealing the right sleeve of his jacket – flat, the cuff stuffed into the pocket. He had no arm.

'So,' said the ragman, 'give me your jacket and I'll give you mine.' Such quiet authority in his voice! The one-armed man took off his jacket. So did the ragman – and I trembled at what I saw: for the ragman's arm stayed in its sleeve, and when the other put it on he had two good arms, thick as tree limbs; but the ragman only had one. 'Go to work,' he said.

After that he found a drunk lying unconscious beneath an army blanket; an old man, hunched, wizened and sick. He took that blanket and wrapped it around himself, but for the drunk, he left new clothes. And now I had to run to keep up with the ragman. Though he was weeping uncontrollably, and bleeding freely at the forehead, pulling his cart with one arm, stumbling for drunkenness, falling again and again, exhausted, old, old and sick, yet he went with terrible speed. On spider's legs he skittered through the alleys of the city, this mile and the next, until he came to its limits and rushed beyond. I wept to see the change in this man. I hurt to see his sorrow. And yet I needed to know what drove him so. The little old ragman – he came to a landfill. He came to the garbage pits. And then I wanted to help him in what he did, but I hung back, hiding. He climbed a hill. With tormented labour he cleared a little space on that hill. Then he sighed. He lay down. He pillowed his head on a handkerchief and a jacket. He covered his bones with an army blanket. And he died.

Oh, how I cried to witness that death! I slumped in a junked car and wailed and mourned as one who had no hope – because I had come to love the ragman. Every other face had paled in the wonder of this man, and I cherished him, but he died. I sobbed myself to sleep.

I did not know – how could I know? – that I slept through Friday night and Saturday and its night too. But then on Sunday morning I was awakened by a violence. Light – pure, hard, demanding light – slammed against my sour face, and I looked, and I saw the last and the first wonder of all. There was the ragman, folding the blanket most carefully, a scar on his forehead, but alive! And, besides that, healthy! There was no sign of sorrow, nor of age, and all the rags that he had gathered shone with cleanliness. Well, then I lowered my head and, trembling for all that I had seen, I myself walked up to the ragman. I told him my name with shame, for I was a sorry figure next to him. Then I took off all my clothes in that place, and I said to him with deep yearning in my voice: 'Dress me.' He dressed me.

My Lord put new rags on me, and I am a wonder beside him.
The ragman, the ragman, the Christ!

Mad, bad or God?

2

Looking at the facts –
historical evidence and sense of the existence of Jesus

Muffins and drinks

Flip chart

Brainstorm different reasons for people not believing in God or Jesus.

Video clip

Indiana Jones and the Last Crusade (1hr 39min 30sec from start, clip runs for 5 min) – point being that believing in God isn't a total blind leap of faith but it does require some faith.

Talk

On the historical evidence and sense of the existence of Jesus (see page 12).

Group time discussion questions

- Mad, bad or God quiz (page 14). Go through and discuss different things.
- Questions:
  - Do you believe in God? Why or why not?
  - Do you believe in Jesus? Why or why not?
  - If someone asked you who Jesus is, what would you say?
  - What evidence do you see of Jesus existing?
  - Have you seen or heard of any miracles – yourself or in your family/friends.
- Write down the questions you have about God and Jesus. Read out and discuss in groups or leave for us to look at later.

Mad, bad or God?

So, how do we know there is a God?

We know we can't see him but there are also a lot of other things we can't see, like electricity or wind, but we still believe they exist. We can see their effects. We can also see the effects of God's existence.

There is also a lot of evidence that God's son, Jesus, existed.

The Bible is not the only book that records the person and actions of Jesus. There are other historical books that mention him.

So, we know he existed as a person.

- He had a body that got tired and hungry
READ: John 4:6 and Matthew 4:2

- He had emotions of anger, love and sadness
READ: Mark 11:15-17, Mark 10:21 and John 11:32-36

- He experienced life! Learning, working, obeying, etc.
READ: Luke 2:46-52, Mark 6:3, Luke 2:51 and Mark 1:13

So, how do we know Jesus was the Son of God?

Anyone could die but who else has come back from the dead three days later?

READ: 1 Corinthians 15:14

So, how do we know that he came back from the dead?

There was no sign of him in the tomb. Other explanations:

- He didn't die
But we know he died. *John 19:34* = a medical sign of death.

- His friends stole his body
What use would a dead body be to his friends?

- Romans stole it!
If the Romans had stolen his body, surely they would have dragged it out when the disciples said, 'he's alive'.

Jesus also appeared to lots of people.
Could it have been a hallucination or a ghost?

But 550+ people saw Jesus on eleven different occasions
over a six-week period.

READ: 1 Corinthians 15:3-7

Mad, bad or God?

Look at the quiz on page 14. Start at the top, reading the
questions in the boxes, and depending on your answers, it
guides you in different directions down the page.

Who do you say Jesus is?

Madman . . .   Thought he was God, but wasn't.

Badman . . .   Knew he wasn't God, out to con people.

God-man . . .   God come to us as a man.

The choice is yours!
READ: John 3:16-17

SO PRAY . . .

Thank God that Christianity is not about a 'blind faith' but it's
a faith based on fact. Ask him to help you to not rely on just
feelings or faith but to base your beliefs on the facts and to
hold on to this when you don't understand it all.

Follow this quiz . . .

⟶ = yes

---▶ = no

START HERE

⬇

Do you think that Jesus really existed?

History
There is so much good evidence, no one really doubts that Jesus existed.

Do you think that Jesus was special?

Do you think that someone made it all up?

Eye-witnesses
Jesus' friends wrote books about him. If they'd exaggerated it, there would have been lots of people around to put them straight.

Do you think Jesus really claimed to be the Son of God?

Do you think the stories about Jesus got exaggerated as time went on?

No U-turn
In the end the Jews took Jesus to court for the crime of blasphemy, which means claiming to be God. Even then he stuck to his claim.

Do you think he really believed what he was saying?

Do you think Jesus' followers wanted to make him into a god against his will?

Do you think Jesus was telling the truth?

Love
Would someone so evil be capable of so much good? And if he knew he was lying, why did he not own up when they were planning to kill him?

Do you think that Jesus was the greatest conman in history?

Do you think that we should do what Jesus said?

Do you think that Jesus was mentally ill, convinced that he was somebody else?

Wisdom
Would someone so 'out-of-it' be capable of some of the wisest words ever spoken on the planet? And what about those miracles?

GOD
The only thing that makes sense is that Jesus was who he said he was. He's what life is all about!

Do you think God cares if we take any notice of him?

Crucial
'If God's there, why doesn't he do something to let us know?' If Jesus told the truth, then God has shown us just what he's like, and we are stupid if we don't hang on his every word.

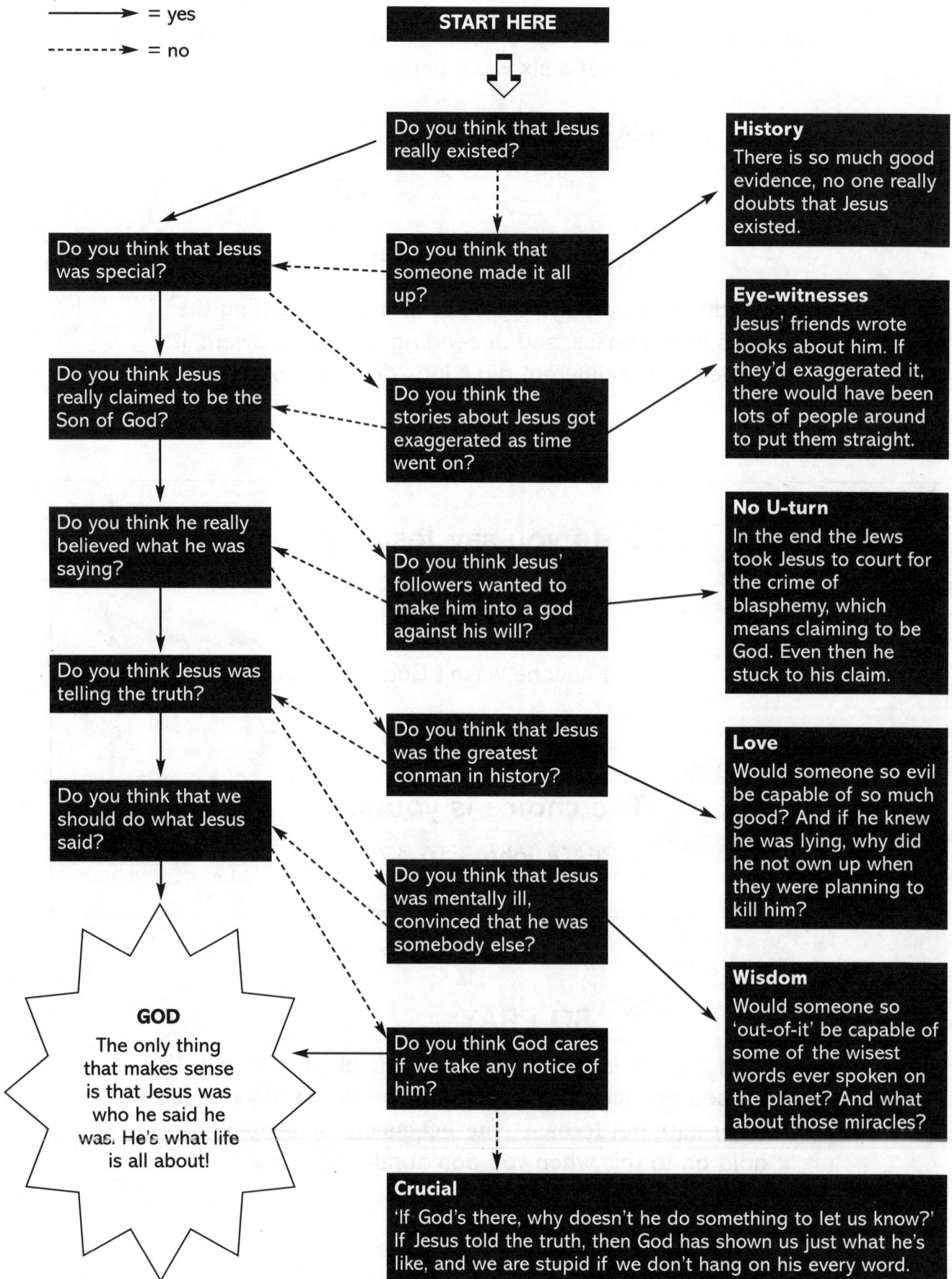

(Taken from *Get God 2000* by World Wide Message Tribe)

Could Jesus have been a cucumber?

3

**Looking at the incarnation of Jesus –
why did he become one of us; what does that mean for us;
a suffering God; the Trinity . . .**

Muffins and drinks

Introduce theme and **brainstorm** on flip-chart human things/experiences/feelings Jesus went through.

Video clip

Show clip from a Crucifixion scene video while playing 'I will love you for the cross', by Matt Redman.

Talk

Talk about God incarnate and so a God who relates to us and who understands.

Group time discussion questions

- Tick-sheet activity (see page 18) – tick things that you can relate to.
- What roles do you play in life? (e.g. sister, student, cousin, etc.) – we all play different roles in life but we are still us in each of these roles.
- Does it help to know that someone understands everything about you?
- Do you often feel misunderstood in life – share times when you have been misunderstood . . .
- Ever heard people say: 'Even if you were the only person on earth Jesus would have died for you so that you could know God?' Do you have trouble believing that? Jesus tells many stories about going after the one. Maybe, read one of these stories in Luke 15?

If time, rejoin as a group and play 'What a friend I've found' by Martin Smith, and pray.

Could Jesus have been a cucumber?

So, why did Jesus have to become human?

We often relate to people like us. The people of Israel had become distant from God because they had disobeyed him. Back in the Old Testament, God used many prophets to warn his people of the consequences of their ungodly lives. Sending Jesus to be one of us was his ultimate expression of love.

Jesus was fully human and fully God . . .
He had a human body.
He had human emotions and he had human experiences.

But was he more than a man?

Jesus said, I am . . .

- the Bread of Life = satisfy our spiritual needs
  READ: John 6:35

- the Light of the World = bring light into our lives
  READ: John 8:12

- the Resurrection and the Life
  READ: John 11:25-26

- the Way, the Truth and the Life = show us the way to God
  READ: John 14:6

Jesus claimed to be the Son of God (John 14:9)
Jesus said he could forgive sins (Mark 2:5)
Jesus said he would judge the world (Matthew 25:31-32)
Even his friends called him: **'My Lord and my God.'**
(John 20:28)

Do you ever say: 'You don't understand me!' to your family? Do you get annoyed when you share a problem with someone and they claim to understand what you are going through? We want to be understood and we want relationships with people – that's what we were created for.

Jesus became human so he *does* understand what it is like to be human – he understands the trials we go through. If Jesus came to earth as anything other than a human we would not relate to him in the way we do when we read/hear about him.

FOR THE CROSS
Matt and Beth Redman

I will love you for the cross,
and I will love you for the cost:
man of sufferings, bringer of my peace.
You came into a world of shame,
and paid the price we could not pay:
death that brought me life, blood that brought me home.
And I love you for the cross, I'm overwhelmed by the mystery.
I love you for the cost,
that Jesus you would do this for me.
When you were broken, you were beaten,
you were punished, I go free.
When you were wounded and rejected,
in your mercy, I am healed.
Jesus Christ, the sinner's friend;
does this kindness know no bounds?
With your precious blood you have purchased me.
O the mystery of the cross, you were punished, you were crushed;
but that punishment has become my peace.
Yes, that punishment has become my peace.

Ever heard people say 'Even if you were the only person on the earth, Jesus would still have died for you so that you could know God'? Do you have trouble believing that? Jesus told many stories about going after just the one . . .
READ: Luke 15

SO PRAY . . .

Thank God that he cared that much about us knowing him and knowing his love that he sent his Son to become one of us – to go through pain and rejection so that he could relate to us and draw us to God. Ask that you would know Jesus as your true friend.

Fully human and fully God

Jesus Christ experienced many feelings and situations.
Look at the list below and tick those you relate to.

- Rejection
- Physical pain
- Abandonment by his friends
- Betrayal
- Persecution – people being down on him because of his faith
- Bullying
- Humiliation
- Torture
- Suffering
- Interrogation (= questioning)
- People talking about him behind his back
- Disapproval
- Personal attack
- Crying
- Sadness
- The death of a friend
- His own death
- Hell
- Temptation
- Abuse
- Being told off
- Arguments
- Being misunderstood
- Anger
- Happiness
- Friendship
- Parties
- Hunger
- Satisfaction
- Tiredness
- Family life
- Love
- Comfort
- Meals with his friends
- Heat/cold
- Work
- Resurrection – being made alive

So has God retired?

4

Looking at what God does now and where he is – the Holy Spirit and why we need him

Muffins and drinks

Ice breaker: Secret angels

Each member of the group (including leaders) writes their name on a piece of paper and drops it into a container. Then each person takes out a name (making sure that no one has picked their own out). It is now their mission to buy a present, write something encouraging, or do a nice thing for that person as anonymously as possible (no one should spend more than £1 on a present). Next time we meet, the gifts are to be given to the leader for them to hand out.

Game

Follow the leader. Get into pairs. Choose one to be the leader and the other to be the follower. Sitting opposite each other, the leader begins by moving slowly . . . perhaps just a hand movement to begin with . . . the follower must copy the leader as if looking in a mirror. Try pulling faces, moving a bit quicker, moving around the room even! What do you notice about being a leader? What do you notice about being a follower? Can you still lead/follow if you are not looking at your partner? Swap over and try it the other way round.

Video

World Wide Message Tribe 'Get God 2000' clip from Week 5.
Talk about the Holy Spirit and what he does today. Various older young people to give testimonies about God at work in their lives and the power of the Holy Spirit.

Group time discussion questions
- Have you ever known anyone's life changed after they became a Christian?
- How have your experiences of God changed you?
- Have you ever had a prayer answered?
- Have you ever felt God with you?
- 'God might have made the world but where is he now?' How would you answer this?
- Have you ever felt the Holy Spirit?
- What would life be like without the Holy Spirit?
- What gifts has God given you? How might you use those gifts to worship him?

So has God retired?

So, what does God do now and where is he?
Jesus didn't just leave us and scoot back up to heaven! He
promised us the Holy Spirit. Throughout the Bible there is talk
of the Holy Spirit and his involvement in creation and in helping
people at particular times for particular tasks. Jesus' power
came from the Holy Spirit and he promised us this Spirit.

READ: John 14:15-30
We are not left alone. Jesus has left us the Holy Spirit to
guide us.

The Bible talks of the fruit of the Spirit.
What does this mean?
A fruit grows if the tree is cared for and watered in the
right way.
If we let the Holy Spirit into our lives and do as he
prompts us,
we will see fruit/results of this.
READ: Galatians 5:22-23

Write below the fruit that you think you could
do with more of in your life . . .

....

....

Have you ever found yourself using the same expressions as
your friends after having spent a few days round each other?
Have you ever said something or acted like your parents and
then discovered that you were imitating their habits without
realising it? We become more like our friends/family
as we are with them.

The more time we spend getting to know God better,
the more we will inherit his character.
God's Spirit helps us to be more like Jesus.

Ephesians 5:1 says:
'Be imitators of God and live a life of love.'

Romans 8 talks about having life through the Spirit.
You might like to read it sometime. It says:

- We need to be controlled by the Spirit not by sinful nature.
  - We are promised eternal life.
  - We are sons and daughters of God.
  - We can know him as a perfect Father.
- We can know we belong to him and are accepted by him.
- We are heirs – he has chosen us to help continue his work
  on earth. He therefore trusts us.
  - Our future is secure.

The Spirit can make these truths known to us.
The Spirit can also help us pray and understand the Bible.

There are also such things as the 'gifts of the Spirit'.
READ: 1 Corinthians 12:1-11

These gifts are given to different people to help them as
Christians and to help them help others. Do you think God
has given you any of these gifts?

God wants us to be filled with the Spirit. We sometimes fill
our lives with other things that limit how much of the Spirit
is evident in us.
If you light a new nightlight candle you will see there is a lot
of wax and a little flame. If you light a used candle you will
see there is a little wax and a larger flame. It's the same with
our lives – we need less of us for there to be more of the
Spirit in us.
READ: Ephesians 4:22-24

**What things do you fill yourself with instead of
God's Spirit?**

Do you want to be more like Jesus? The Holy Spirit can help
you. In your groups share your experience/understanding of
the Holy Spirit with each other.

SO PRAY . . .

Thank God that he did not leave us as orphans but has
adopted us into his family and has left us his Spirit to guide
and comfort us. Ask him to fill you with his Spirit and that you
would see the fruit of this. Perhaps, ask what things are
getting in the way of the Spirit in your life.

Don't doubt in the dark what you knew in the light (5)

Holding on to the truth – where to find the truth: looking at the Bible

Muffins and drinks

Icebreaker game

Blindfold two volunteers and get them to smell, feel and taste various foods and guess what they are.

Video clip

The Truman Show (59min 30sec from start – the clip runs for 7min 23sec).
(Point – we sometimes prefer to be satisfied with less than the whole truth.)

Speak on constant truths. (To include sleepwalking antics and video clip explanations.)

Video clip

The Truman Show (1hr 19min 30sec from start – the clip runs for 13min 8sec).
(Point – it took the boat to go through the sky for Truman to realise the truth. Sometimes we need to experience God in a dynamic way for us to believe in him and we must hold on to these times when things seem hard or complicated. We know the sun is there even if it is not shining.)

Group time discussion questions

The point of this time is to understand that some things are constant and that truth is always true. Like when you know your way around your bedroom in the light you also know your way in the dark.

- Does your mum/dad/guardian love you less when they are angry with you?
- Do you stop caring for your pet if it does wrong?
- How do you know Russia exists?
- Have you or anyone you know ever walked in their sleep? Share stories.
- Remember a time when you were sure Christianity was true. Why were you sure?
- Write a psalm: hand out pieces of paper and pens (see page 26). Explain how to write a psalm. They take the structure: 'Lord I feel . . . But I know . . . So I will . . .' It is a personal thing and up to each person to write down how they feel to God, and then what they know about God and so what they will do as a result. Most of the Psalms in the Bible take this form. The point is how we feel changes but what is true about God stays constant so we must hold these things in balance. Ask people to read what they have written (if they want to).

Don't doubt in the dark what you knew in the light

When things go wrong is it easy to believe that God does not care? Jesus said:

'I am the way and the truth and the life. No one comes to the Father except through me.'
(John 14:6)
But how do we know what the truth is and which way to go?

The Psalmist said:
'Your word is a lamp to my feet and a light for my path.'
(Psalm 119:105)
The Bible is God's word – we can find the truth in here.

Our feelings do not alter what is true – we must hold on to the truth of who God is and what he has done for us and what he wants to do for us. Someone once described it as a train:

Fact	Faith	Feeling
God and his Word the Bible	Our trust in God and his Word	The results of trusting God

(from *Knowing God Personally*, 2001)

The engine must pull the carriages. The carriages would not be able to pull the train. In the same way our faith and our feelings cannot be totally trusted because these come and go. It is important to rely on God and what he said in the Bible, and not be pushed around by our feelings. Just as the coal needs to be put into the engine from the coal truck in order for the train to run, so we need to put our trust in God's word – the truth.

The Bible says:
'Jesus Christ is the same yesterday and today and for ever.'
(Hebrews 13:8)

24

Jesus does not change. We can trust him. We can trust what the Bible says. We can choose to accept what the Bible says – what God says. We can choose to accept the truth.

In the film *The Matrix* there is a clip where Morpheus offers Neo two pills. The red pill represents the truth and the blue pill will send him back and it will be as if nothing had happened – he will continue living with the wool pulled over his eyes, disguising the truth. We have to choose to accept the truth even if it is different from what our friends and family might think/believe.

Circumstances can so easily cloud the truth but we must hold on to the truth and remember that our lives and the world around us change but Jesus never changes. He is the same yesterday, today and tomorrow.

CAN'T GIVE UP NOW
Mary Mary

Listen to the words of 'Can't give up now' by Mary Mary, released on the Columbia label by Sony Music, catalogue no. 4979852.

SO PRAY . . .

That you would base your faith on the truth – that despite your circumstances you will know and believe the truth in God's Word – the Bible.

Write a Psalm . . .

'Lord, I feel . . .
But I know . . . So I will . . .'

Why's the world so messed up?

Looking at evil and issues such as the occult and the way the devil works

Muffins and drinks

Icebreaker: taste game

Have a number of different samples of cola and get people to guess which is the genuine Coca-Cola and which are copies (see page 28). (The devil copies, he can't create.)

Video clip

Bedazzled (9min 15sec into film for 5min 30sec) – the devil is attractive and lures us. Not made up – the devil offers us things we want.

Speak

On evil, the devil and testify of experiences.

Listen to song 'Dear Lie' by TLC (from *Fanmail* album, released on the Arista label by BMG, catalogue no. 73008260552).

Get people to think about what the words mean to them. The devil is the father of lies and cannot be trusted.

Group time discussion questions

- Do you know people who have been involved in occult practices?
- Do you know people who have played with a Ouija board?
- If you were your own enemy how would you attack you?
- Have you ever been tricked into doing something you didn't want to do?

Pray

Coca-Cola Challenge

Taste the five samples of cola and write down the number on the glass next to the type you think it is.

Type	Number
Coca-Cola	
Virgin Cola	
Pepsi	
Tesco Value Cola	
Sainsbury's Economy Cola	

Why's the world so messed up?

So what about the devil? How do we know he exists?

- The Bible speaks about him – 1 Peter 5:8-11
  - Our own experience of being tempted.
- Common sense when you look at the world.

The Bible says the devil is the father of lies (John 8:44).
His main aim is to wreck your life.
He tries to stop people believing in Jesus, he tempts us, he makes us doubt and he accuses us, saying: 'You're not good enough.' He knows our weak points and attacks these.

Why are people interested in evil?

We all have some kind of spiritual thirst. John 6:35 says how we were made with a built-in need for God. We try to quench that thirst in many different ways. We can focus spiritually on God or the devil. The devil may appear to offer us what God can but he is the father of lies – he cannot be trusted.

What is the occult?

Occult = hidden things
If we get involved in occult practices it means taking a step into hidden things – it means going where we were never meant to be.
When you mess about in occult things, sooner or later those things will mess about with you.

The devil may be stronger than us, but he's no match for Jesus.

READ: Colossians 2:15

The devil was defeated on the cross – Jesus has already won!

> **When the devil reminds you of your past, remind him of his future.**

The results of encounters with unwholesome spiritual forces are often depression, suicidal tendencies and compulsive behaviour. That is why God tells us not to get dragged into occult practices . . . mediums, white/black magic, tarot, spells, channelling, Ouija boards . . .
all are trouble.

How can I resist evil then?

If you've been into occult stuff, you need to turn your back on it.
Get rid of anything linked with that activity, i.e. charms, videos, books, cards, etc. Say sorry to God and ask him to clean you up and to fill you with his Holy Spirit.
The Bible talks of putting on the armour of God to be protected from the devil:

Ephesians 6:10-18
Belt = knowing the truth about God
Breastplate = being made clean by God
Shoes = being ready to tell others about Jesus
Shield = trusting God
Helmet = salvation: you belong to Jesus
Sword = the Bible: it's a powerful weapon

Three points to remember:
• We should not be fascinated by the devil
• We must not forget that he exists (John 10:10)
• We must not fear him (1 John 4:18)

SO PRAY . . .

Ask Jesus to lift you out of dark things into his light: into freedom, forgiveness and life. Ask him to help you remember that the devil has no hold over you now that you belong to Jesus. Perhaps, use the armour in Ephesians 6 as a daily prayer for protection.

Everything else is rubbish ⑦

Looking at the stuff we use to replace God and how that never satisfies

Muffins and drinks

Icebreaker game

Remember tray

Video clip

Muppets in Space (27min 49sec from start – the clip runs for 3min 28sec) – he gave up everything (even his reputation) to find what he knew was true.

Speak

On putting God first.

Group time discussion questions

- If there was a fire in your house, what three things would you save?

- Have you ever had hobbies or collected stuff you'd do anything for/to get?

- What one thing couldn't you do without? What if you had to give it up? How would you feel?

- Read: Philippians 3:7-9 from The Youth Bible version (see page 34). Discuss.

- Do the plant/tree activity (see page 33).

Everything else is rubbish

But whatever was to my profit I now consider loss for the sake of Christ. What is more, I consider everything a loss compared to the surpassing greatness of knowing Christ Jesus my Lord, for whose sake I have lost all things. I consider them rubbish, that I may gain Christ and be found in him . . . (Philippians 3:7-9)

If you are a Christian, do you think your priorities have changed since becoming a Christian?

. . . .

Do you think they should?

. . . .

Read the following words of this Psalm:

> How lovely is your dwelling place,
> O Lord Almighty!
> My soul yearns, even faints,
> for the courts of the Lord;
> my heart and my flesh cry out
> for the living God . . .
> . . . Better is one day in your courts
> than a thousand elsewhere;
> I would rather be a doorkeeper in the
> house of my God
> than dwell in the tents of the wicked . . .
> (Psalm 84)
> 1-2, 10-

What do you think it means?

. . . .

Do you agree with it?

....

Would you like to agree with it?

....

Throughout the Old Testament God is angry and jealous for his people who are making gods of things.

You shall not make for yourself an idol in the form of anything in heaven above or on the earth beneath or in the waters below. You shall not bow down to them or worship them; for I, the Lord your God, am a jealous God . . . (Exodus 20:4-5)

What things do you put before God/make an idol of?
These things are like a forest blocking our view of God. On a blank sheet of paper, draw these things as trees or plants – depending on importance/size of problem. See below:

Me   image   time   drinking   shopping   GOD

SO PRAY . . .

Give the things you have drawn to God and pray that he would help you to put him first in your life. Ask God to help you keep life in perspective and to help you keep the forests cut down. Thank God that he is persistent in trying to get our attention.

Those things were important to me,
but now I think they are worth nothing
because of Christ. Not only those
things, but I think that **all things are
worth nothing compared with the
greatness of knowing Christ Jesus
my Lord**. Because of him, I have lost all
those things, and now I know they are
worthless rubbish. This allows me to
have Christ and to belong to him. Now
I am right with God, not because
I followed the law, but because
I believed in Christ. God uses my faith
to make me right with him.

Philippians 3:7-9

So what next?

8

How do we go on as Christians? Looking at how to know God more, not just know about him . . .
e.g. Church, fellowship, prayer, etc.

Muffins and drinks

Icebreaker

The Chocolate Game

'Square challenge'

You must create your square with the same colour pieces but you do not have all the pieces. Everyone else has to do the same but all have the same problem that they do not have what they need on their own. You are not allowed to take or ask for other people's pieces. The only thing you can do is give yours to other people. The first person to complete their square wins!

Video clip

Clip from series *My So-called Life* episode 'Guardian Angel' – show first 4min 55sec or show a clip from *The Simpsons* when they go to church. Explain how to many, church is irrelevant even when it should be most relevant (like at Christmas) but that many just do not give it a chance or understand what church really is (people not building).

Speak

On praying, reading the Bible and going to church.

Group time discussion questions

• Which soap operas/bands are you into? You know about them but do you know them?

• What would Christmas be like without your family?

• What do you like best about church?

• What would your perfect church be like – draw or write.

• Do text message challenge (see page 39).

So what next?

So what should I do if I want to be a Christian?

The ABC of starting over
(adapted from *Get God 2000*)

A is for admit
We can't just cruise up to the almighty as if we're the business. If you want to be a Christian, you've got to admit that you've done loads of stuff wrong, and want to say sorry. You need to be ready, with God's help, to sack every wrong action, word and thought that you know he doesn't like, and start all over again.

B is for believe
It's pretty obvious, but if you want to be a Christian, you've got to believe in Jesus and trust that when he died on the cross, he was taking the punishment for all the wrong things you've ever done.

C is for consider
Being a Christian isn't the soft option – you need to think it through before making a choice you might regret. If you give everything to God, people will think you're a bit weird. It will cost you time and energy to be a real Christian. But in return you'll get the fullest life now, and eternal life in paradise when you die.

D is for do it
If you know it's true, there's no point dilly-dallying about. Go for it. You are not a Christian because you know the facts about Jesus – you've actually got to do something about it. At 10 Downing Street (where the Prime Minister lives) there is no door handle or lock on the outside of the door – the only way in is if someone opens the door from the inside. It's the same with Jesus – we have to open our lives, our hearts and let him in.

Jesus said this:

'Here I am, I stand at the door and knock. If anyone hears my voice and opens the door, I will come in.'

Some people pray a prayer to ask Jesus to come into their life. You may have done this before but if you want to re-commit you can also pray this prayer. Only pray it if you really mean it:

Lord Jesus, I want to follow you. I know I've done loads of bad things. I know I don't deserve to go to heaven. I'm sorry and I turn away from everything I know is wrong in my life. Thank you so much for dying in my place. Please fill me with your Holy Spirit. With your help, I'll live all out for you for the rest of my life. Amen.

So what do people do?

Three really important things you can do to keep your friendship going with Jesus are to pray, read the Bible and go to church.

• *Pray*
We pray to our Father in heaven,
in Jesus' name and with the help of the Holy Spirit.
God answers prayer by saying 'yes', 'no' or 'wait'.
Jesus gave us a prayer to pray called the Lord's Prayer
You can find it in: **Matthew 6:5-13.**

Try to pray regularly and not just when things are bad!
Read: 1 Thessalonians 5:17 & Ephesians 6:18

• *Read the Bible*
The Bible is God's word to us. The Bible was written by people but was inspired by God. It is our manual for life and by reading it we can find out what to believe and how to live. It doesn't give us all the answers but does give us guidelines and God can speak to us through it.

READ: Matthew 4:4 & 2 Timothy 3:16
Reading the Bible helps us . . .
- Become like Jesus (2 Corinthians 3:18)
- Have joy and peace (Psalm 23:5)
- Receive guidance (Psalm 119:105)
- Receive healing (Proverbs 4:20-22)
- Be protected (Matthew 4:1-11)
- Come under God's power (Hebrews 4:12)
- Get cleaned up (John 15:3)

- *Go to church*
It is good to be surrounded by other believers –
we can encourage and learn from each other. Jesus said:
**'For where two or three come together in my name,
there I am with them.'**
(Matthew 18:20)

The Bible calls the church a family: **Galatians 6:10**
Christians are brothers and sisters to each other.
God is the head of this family.

The Bible also calls the church a body: **Romans 12:4-8**
The body is made up of many different parts but they all work together to
function properly. God wants us to work together in things. We may not like all
the people in our new family but we must still learn to love them. Even when
they annoy us we must still love them and encourage each other.

READ: Ephesians 2:19-22
We, the Church, have Jesus holding us together (v20)
and the Holy Spirit living in us (v22).

The church is the people, not the building.

SO PRAY . . .

Thank God that he doesn't make us do all this on our own. Ask him to help you
pray and read your Bible. Ask him to help you be committed to the church and
to learn to get on with your new family.

Rewrite the Lord's Prayer in text format in the screen below.
You can only use 160 characters.
Compare with your group.

Only u can be u

9

Looking at purpose and living as God would want you to

Muffins and drinks

Icebreaker

Play charades.

Impressions

Get people to share any impressions they can do and get everyone to guess who they are.

Video clip

Mrs Doubtfire clip, 45min 45sec from start – the clip lasts 6min 33sec.

The point being that although he impersonated the nanny very well he could not hold up the disguise for long as he could not totally hide who he was and he found it hard trying to be more than one person at a time.

Speak on knowing who you are as a child of God

(to include a short clip from *The Lion King*, 1hr 15sec into film – clip runs for 5min).

Group time discussion questions

- Write something nice about everyone in the group anonymously on pieces of paper.
- Read the 'You Are Very Special' poem (see page 43).
- If you could be anyone else for a day who would you be and why?
- What would be bad about being them?
- What makes you unique?
- What three things do you want to do or say you were like before you die?

Only u can be u

So what can I do? What use am I to God?

Do you ever feel insignificant? Like you can't make a difference?
You may only be one drop in the ocean but the ocean is made up of many drops.

The starfish story

A man was taking a walk along the beachfront when he saw a young boy picking up starfish one by one and throwing them back into the waters. The tide had washed up thousands of starfish and they were set to die unless back in the water. The man went up to the young boy and said, 'What are you doing? Can you not see how many starfish there are on the sand? You will never be able to save them all! What's the point? What difference are you going to make?' The boy answered, 'Well, I'm sure it made a difference to this one!' as he picked up another starfish and threw it back into the sea.

Do you look at life like this? Do you think that you are special and that God created you for a purpose?

READ: Jeremiah 29:11

No one can be you and no one can do things in exactly the same way you do. Read this poem and discuss how it makes you feel . . .

YOU ARE VERY SPECIAL!

In all the world there is nobody,
nobody like you.
Since the beginning of time there has never been another person like
you. Nobody has your smile, your eyes, your hands or your hair.
Nobody owns your handwriting or your voice.
YOU'RE SPECIAL!
Nobody can paint your brush strokes.
Nobody has your taste for food or music, or dance or art.
Nobody in all the universe sees the things as you do.
In all the time there has never been
anyone who laughs in exactly the same way – so – YOU'RE SPECIAL!
You're different from any other person
who has ever lived in the history of the universe.
You are the only one in the whole of Creation who has
your particular set of abilities.
There is always someone who is better at one thing or another.
Every person is your superior in at least one way.
Nobody in the universe can reach the quality or combination of your
talents, your feelings.
Like a roomful of musical instruments some might excel in one way or
another, but nobody can
match the symphonic sound when all are played together – your
symphony.
Through all eternity no one will ever walk, talk or think or do exactly
like you.
YOU'RE SPECIAL!
You're rare and in all rarity there
is enormous value. Because of your great value,
the need for you to imitate anyone else is absolutely wrong.
YOU'RE SPECIAL!
And it is no accident you are.
Please realise that God made you for a special purpose.
He has a job for you to do that nobody else can do as well as you can.
Out of the billion of applicants only one is qualified.
Only one has the unique and right combination of what it takes.
And that one is YOU!

YOU'RE SPECIAL!!!!

So what gifts/talents do you think you have?
Write them below . . .

....

....

You could spend a lifetime comparing yourself with others and wishing you were someone else. But life is not a rehearsal – don't waste it and don't waste yourself and all the talents God has given you.

God created you. He created you in his image.
Read this Psalm:

Psalm 139:13-16

We need to learn to love ourselves.
The Bible says our bodies are temples of the Holy Spirit:

READ: 1 Corinthians 6:19-20

What do you think this means?

In your groups go round and say one positive thing about each person – you may like to write these down. Learn to build on your qualities and not always focus on your mistakes. You are you and you need to learn to love you. It's not an overnight thing but God wants to help you love yourself.

If you think you are no use for God, ask him what it is he wants you to do. We all are unique – as no snowflake is the same, we are also all different. And as Christians we need to work together and use these differences together. Remember the Body of Christ illustration (see **1 Corinthians 12:12-31**)? One snowflake may melt on your cheek but enough snowflakes together and they can stop traffic!

SO PRAY . . .

Thank God for making you, you. Pray that God would help you learn to love you and also to use the gifts he has given you to bless him.

10

Go!

Looking at evangelism – why, how, when . . .

Muffins and drinks

Icebreaker

'Pictionary with a difference' . . . Get into teams and have flip-charts as paper, chocolate spread as ink and draw specified words as pictures but using noses or other parts of the face.

Video clips   29:02 – 38:50

Show a clip of a nutty and over-the-top evangelist (*Leap of Faith*, 29min into film for 10min 16sec) and then show a clip from *Sister Act 1* where they are doing community work (51min 38sec into film for 9min) . . . the point being to show how not to and how to – actions speak louder and how you speak is important (i.e. not shouting hell and damnation at people!).

Testimonies

All leaders to share examples of 'effective' evangelism – not necessarily leading to conversion.

Drama

Divide the young people up into groups and ask them to read Peter's denial of Jesus in Matthew 14:66-72. Ask them to create a modern-day version of this and what it is like to be a Christian at school or home. Perform short dramas to the rest of the group.

Group time discussion questions

- Do your friends know that you are a Christian or that you go to church?
- What do your friends think of you because of this?
- Do you find it easy to share what you believe with them?
- Do you pray for your friends?
- What do you worry about when it comes to telling your friends about Jesus?
- What have you learnt/found good about the course?
- All write down these things to be given in at end.
- What do you want for future meetings?
- Pray.

Go!

Why and how should I tell others?

If you believe Jesus is the truth then he's got to be true for everyone. You can't keep him to yourself. When Mary had Jesus she knew she couldn't keep him to herself, like another mother might. She knew he was the Son of God so she had to let go.

In the parables that Jesus tells in Luke 15 there is so much joy when what was 'lost' is found.

When she finds it, she will call her friends and neighbours and say, 'Be happy with me because I have found the coin that I lost.' (Luke 15:9)

What worries you about telling your friends?

....

....

....

Why?

READ: Matthew 28:19-20

Why did you become a Christian? Try writing your personal story here. It doesn't have to be 'dramatic' – just write what and who influenced your decision. It might have been a gradual change or you might know the moment you made that step. It's all valid and it's all your story.

....

....

....

....

I'm being myself in Jesus and he's being himself in me.

How?

- Just be friendly with people – be yourself
- Be honest
- Be ready to answer friends' questions
- Don't hide the fact you are a Christian
- Don't be afraid to not know all the answers
- Don't just talk at people – your actions will speak louder than your words

Pray, pray and pray some more!

You are not alone . . .

READ: Mark 13:11

Sometimes it can feel like we are on trial when people question us about our faith. But God is with us and his Holy Spirit can help us know what to say.

READ: Luke 8:16-18

Read the Vision (page 48). It is quite old and may seem slightly over the top but it is true in many ways. Does it inspire you or make you understand the importance of telling others any more?

SO PRAY . . .

Pray for all those you know who aren't Christians yet. Perhaps you could commit to praying for a few people each day – ask God who these might be. Ask God to give you boldness in sharing your faith and ask him to give you opportunities.

Thank him that he saved you.

A Vision of the Lost

William Booth

On a recent journey I found myself thinking about the multitudes around me. They were living carelessly in the most open and shameless rebellion against God, without a thought for their eternal welfare. As I looked out of the coach window, I seemed to see them all . . . millions of people given up to their drink, pleasure, dancing and their music, their business, anxieties, politics and troubles. Ignorant – wilfully ignorant in many cases – and in other instances knowing all about the truth and not caring at all. Suddenly, as I thought about them I had a vision.

In it I saw a dark and stormy ocean over which black clouds hung heavily. Every now and then vivid lightning flashed and loud thunder rolled, while the winds drove foaming waves into a tempest that was claiming lives. There were millions cursing, struggling and drowning and as I watched, some of them sank to rise no more. Then I noticed a mighty rock that rose up out of the dark angry ocean. Its summit towered high above the black clouds and all around its base I saw a vast platform. Onto this platform, I saw with delight that a number of the poor struggling wretches were continually climbing out of the angry ocean. And I saw a few of these who were already safe on the platform helping others onto the rock. Many were working with ladders, ropes and boats to rescue those who were drowning. Occasionally someone actually jumped into the water, regardless of the consequences, in their passion to 'rescue the perishing'.

I hardly knew which sight delighted me more – the sight of the people rescued, or the devotion and self-sacrifice of those who rescued them. Looking more closely, I realised that the people on the platform were quite a mixed company. They occupied themselves in different ways. Some spent their days trading whilst others amused themselves by dressing up for the admiration of their peers. Many were chiefly concerned with eating and drinking and yet others were taken up with arguing about the people that had already been rescued. Only very few of them made it their business to rescue people from the sea.

What puzzled me most was the fact that although all of them had been rescued from the ocean at one time or other, nearly everyone seemed to have forgotten about it. And what seemed equally strange was that they did not seem to care about the people who were drowning right before their eyes – many of whom were their own spouses, brothers and sisters and even their own children.

Those on the rock had received a call from the one who had himself gone down into the sea. They'd heard his voice and felt they ought to obey it – or at least so they said. They professed to love him and to sympathise with him in the task he had undertaken. But they were so distracted by their professions, pleasures and their preparation for going to the mainland, that they did not help him. So the multitude went on right before them, struggling, shrieking and drowning in the darkness.

And then I noticed that some of the people on the platform were crying out to him to come to them! Many wanted him to spend his time and strength in making them happier. Others wanted him to take away various doubts and misgivings they had concerning the truth of some letters he had written to them. Some wanted him to make them feel more secure in the rock – so secure that they would be quite sure that they would never slip off again into the ocean. So they would meet and, climbing high on the rock, they would cry, 'Come to us! Come to help us!' And all the while he was down in the sea trying to rescue them and looking to those on the rock for help. And then I understood it all.

The sea was the ocean of human existence. The lightning was the piercing truth coming from Jehovah's throne. The thunder was the distant echoing of God's wrath. The multitudes struggling in the stormy sea were 'the lost', ungodly people of every kindred, tongue and nation. That great sheltering rock represented Calvary, the place where Jesus had died for them. And the people on it were those who had been rescued. The handful of determined ones that risked their lives to save the perishing were the true soldiers of the cross. The one calling on the rescued to help him rescue others was Jesus himself.

Fellow Christians, you have been rescued from the waters, yet he is still in the sea calling for your help. Don't be deceived by appearances – men and things are not what they seem. All who are not on the rock are in the sea!

Jesus is in the midst of the dying multitude, struggling to save them. He wants you to jump in and help. Will you jump or will you linger on the bank, singing and praying about perishing souls? Lay aside your shame, your cares about the opinions of others and all the selfish loves that have held you back for so long, and rush to the rescue of these dying men and women.

Unquestionably the surging sea is dark and dangerous. The leap means difficulty, scorn and suffering for everyone who takes it. Yet he who beckons you from the sea knows what it will mean – and knowing, he still bids you to come.

You have enjoyed your Christianity long enough. Going down among the perishing crowds is your duty. From now on your ease will depend on sharing their pain and your heaven in going into the very jaws of hell to rescue them.

Now what will you do?

Know what is really true, not what is nearly true

Weekend away somewhere . . .

A WEEKEND AWAY – VENUE AND DATE TO BE DECIDED

TIME TO GO DEEPER INTO ISSUES RAISED IN THIS COURSE, TO MAKE FRIENDS AND HAVE SOME FUN.

MORE INFORMATION TO COME . . .

Look in detail about image/devil/acceptance. Maybe use films such as *The Matrix* and *Bedazzled*. Have a chilled-out time with plenty of prayer, talks and practical suggestions/discussion.

See example holiday programme (based on actual holiday) on pages 52-62.

Weekend Programme

FRIDAY

Arrive:	4pm	Sort out rooms and settle in – refreshments
	5pm	Introduction to weekend Challenge – teamwork game (see page 56)
	7pm	Dinner
	7.45pm	Activities: Icebreaker Jenga/ Handicapped obstacle course Big group time – intro to theme Small group time (theme = friends)
	9pm	Dance mat/PlayStation/karaoke contest
	10.30pm	Film – with refreshments
	Midnight	Bed
	1am	Night BBQ – toasting marshmallows (This will be a surprise – we will wake them up)

SATURDAY

8am	Wake up
9am	Breakfast (team A to prepare)
10am	Wide game – 'Grab their flag'
11am	Activities: Bin-liner designer/Make a face Big group time – intro to theme Small group time (theme = image)
1pm	Lunch (team B to prepare)
1.45pm	Sports game
2.15pm	Game: playing-cards hunt
2.45pm	Dance mat/PlayStation/Karaoke contest
4pm-8pm	Guest speaker to organise wide games and talk (theme – self-worth)
6pm	Dinner
8pm	Small groups – plan contribution to service
9.30pm	Dance mat/PlayStation/Karaoke contest
10pm	'Spotlight' wide game Film
Midnight	Bed

SUNDAY

8am	Wake up
9am	Breakfast (Team C to prepare)
10am	Free time
11am	Service – talk, drama, worship, call to go deeper with God and choose 'red pill'. Group's contribution to service.
12 noon	. . . *Yeah and?* – week 10 'Evangelism' Game
1pm	Lunch Clear up rooms and lodge in groups Discussion in groups
2.30pm	Awards and thank-you's
3pm	HOME

Theme: Friends

Friday pm

ACTIVITIES

Big Jenga challenge

Each block has a question on it (some simple, some more revealing!) and as each player takes it in turn to pull a block out they must answer that question. Points given for honesty! Points deducted if tower falls down! The idea is that people get to know each other better.

Handicapped obstacle course

Teams must compete against each other to complete a relay obstacle course (i.e. another member starts when other finishes) but each person is given a specified handicap (see page 57). Points deducted for cheating!

BIG GROUP TIME

Situation dramas

Two dramas performed about 'situations' within friendships (see pages 58 and 59) – ask for show of hands for which resolution they would take.

SMALL GROUP TIME

- Each come up with an acronym for the word 'friends' (i.e. F = faithful, R = reliable, I = interesting and so on . . .). Each do one on a piece of paper trying to draw out the qualities that make a good friend.
- Share stories of when you have been let down by friends (how it made you feel, etc.) and when you have had a friend stand by you or be nice to you.
- Bible passages: Proverbs (two are better than one)
- Play song: 'You've got a friend' by Brand New Heavies or 'What a friend I've found' by Delirious.

CHALLENGE: TEAMWORK

Four people in a team, tied together by their wrists – one young leader to go with them to show them where the next challenge is.

1. Find the key – hidden in the room are three keys with a clue attached to them. They must hunt around and then tie the key to someone's wrist that's in the middle of the line (they cannot untie the key).
   GO

2. Rubber duck pond – three of the ducks have a clue attached to them. The group must fish the ducks out using the rod provided and standing straight upright (so not bending nearer to the pool) until they find a duck with a clue on.
   OUTSIDE

3. Cobweb maze (or obstacle course) – the group must climb through the cobweb to get to the cashboxes on the windowsill and find their clue in one of the cashboxes by using their key.
   AND

4. Star gazing – the group must enter the pitch-black room and find a star with a clue underneath it (which will be under a flap of paper).
   LOOK

5. Steady hand – the group must complete the steady hand tests without a beep, at the same time as each other. On completion they will receive a clue.
   UP

The clues they collect should tell them where to find the prize. There are only enough prizes for one group so it is a race against each other involving teamwork, patience and ability. They must have all the clues to receive the prize – so they can't just guess the location of the prize. The prize is to be hanging from a tree.

HANDICAPPED OBSTACLE COURSE

- You only have one leg. Hold the other one up behind you at all times (you may occasionally switch your 'good' leg for comfort).

- You don't have a right arm. Hold it behind you at all times, and don't use it for anything (pretend it doesn't exist).

- You don't have arms at all. Hold them both behind your back and don't use them for anything (pretend they don't exist).

- You are blind. Get a blindfold from the leader and wear it at all times. Keep your eyes closed too, and don't try to peek.

- You have no use of your legs. Yeah, they're there, but you can't move them at all. You can't stand on them or flex the muscles at all.

- You have no knee or elbow joints – they're just missing! This makes movement very difficult, and climbing almost impossible. Your legs and arms must remain stiff at all times.

- You cannot walk, you can only run. You can stand still, or you can run. That's it.

- You can't stand on your feet, you must walk on your knees.

- You are a baby and can only crawl on all fours.

- You are a little back to front and can only walk backwards.

- You are an extremely happy person and skip everywhere!

- You are emotionally unstable, and have an irrational need to shout 'EEEK!' every five seconds.

SITUATIONS

Act out the two situations and after each one have the young people discuss the questions in small groups, then give a report back.

SITUATION 1

(Sharon is on the phone to her friend Lisa.)

Sharon   Hi, Lisa! It's Sharon here! Are you coming to my party on Saturday?

Lisa   Oops! I knew there was something I'd forgotten about!

Sharon   What do you mean?

Lisa   Well, it's just that this lad called Mike from year 10 has asked me to go out to the cinema with him on Saturday. I've never been out on a date before.

Sharon   Do you mean you're not coming to my party?

Lisa   Sorry, but I can't.

Sharon   *(Angrily)* Well, that's just great! You're my best friend and don't even want to come to my party. What am I supposed to do? It won't be much of a party if nobody comes. I suppose you want me to cancel everything just so that you can go and snog some guy you've never met before. Some friend you are!

Lisa   But Sharon, you don't understand.

Sharon   Well don't expect me to come out with you from now on. I'll find some better friends else-where. *(Slams phone down)*

Question: **If you were Sharon, what would you do?**

- Go ahead with the party and ignore Lisa from now on.
- Say sorry to Lisa and change the date of your party.
- Invite Lisa and Mike to your party.
- Try and stop Lisa going out with Mike.
- Something else (what?).

SITUATION 2

(John and Darren are at the football match.)

John	COME ON YOU REDS! This is the best match I've seen all season!
Darren	*(Miserable)* Huh! Suppose so!
John	What's wrong, Darren? You've been miserable all day.
Darren	Look, I don't want to talk about it, all right?
John	Come on! I'm your best mate – you can tell me.
Darren	Promise you won't tell anyone?
John	Of course.
Darren	Well, you know that £5 you lost last week, I took it.
John	*(Shocked)* You took it? You saw me looking for it, it meant I couldn't go to that concert and I really got done for it.
Darren	My brother made me do it, honest!
John	You're a criminal! My best mate's a criminal! I can't have everybody thinking I hang around with criminals! How could you do this to me?
Darren	I knew you wouldn't understand if I confessed to you. I'll save up and give it back, John.
John	Well what am I supposed to do? You're just a waster, Darren, and unless you sort yourself out you might as well forget hanging around with me.

Question:	**If you were John, what would you do?**
	• Tell Darren to get lost.
	• Give Darren one more chance, and ditch him if he does something else wrong.
	• Tell your parents it was Darren, knowing they'd hate him for life.
	• Stick with Darren and make him pay back the £5.
	• Forget about the whole incident.

Theme: Image   Saturday am

ACTIVITIES

Bin-liner designer

Each team chooses a model; give them each a few bin bags, some plastic bags, some sticky tape, scissors and a hairdryer. They have five minutes in which to dress their model in an appropriate outfit. When the time is up their models must parade down the catwalk to music and they will be judged on creativity, style and charisma!

Make a face

Each team must choose another model and they have five minutes to create a face using face paints. The model must parade down the catwalk to music and they will be marked on creativity, effect and imagination!

BIG GROUP TIME

- Video clip from *Clueless* showing how obsessed some people can get with image/appearance.
- Visual talk using teddy bear (see page 61).

SMALL GROUP TIME

- Questions:
  - What wouldn't you be seen dead in?
  - What is the worst item of clothing you have worn or been given?
  - Have you ever been teased for how you looked?
  - How did it make you feel?
  - Have you ever teased others?
- Draw a caricature of yourself – do you think this is how God sees you?
- Bible passage: Man looks at outside, God looks at heart.

MASKED TEDDY

Before the meeting, find a teddy bear and wrap its head up with various 'masks', as follows:

- Wrap the head in a sheet of brown paper
- On top of this, wrap round a layer of toilet paper
- On top of this, wrap a layer of newspaper
- On top of this, wrap a layer of silver foil
- On top of this, wrap a layer of glossy paper with bright pictures from magazines.

Wrap them so each layer can be pulled off the head in turn, leaving the others in place.

Talk

Say that one of the things about wearing fashionable or trendy clothes is that we are creating an image – we want to look good, so that other people notice us and appreciate us, so we dress up in the latest fashions or wear designer label clothes. Now there is nothing wrong with wanting to look nice, but becoming obsessed by it or being ruled by fashion rather than choosing what we like is wrong. The image we try and show to other people is often very different from the 'real me' – many of us try to hide ourselves behind a false image, a bit like putting on a mask.

Briefly explain some of the false images or masks that people wear; introduce your teddy who's going to help illustrate the talk, and bring out your teddy (with the top layer of glossy pictures showing). Take each layer off in turn, explaining which image it represents.

The glossy paper is the 'All Right' mask – this represents people who are always 'all right', with no problems at all. Usually, people wearing this mask are hiding all the problems and things that are wrong with their life, because they are afraid others wouldn't like them if they knew what they were really like.

The silver foil layer represents people who wear the 'Ice Cool' mask. These are people who like to create an image of being cold or really 'hard' – the tough guy or tough girl, who doesn't need anyone to help them – they can stand up for themselves. Unfortunately, this is just a mask – people who act tough are usually lonely or hurting inside, and desperately wanting someone to love them and care for them. The problem with being 'Ice Cool' is that you never let other people close enough to know the real you and love you for what you are.

The newspaper layer is the 'Show Off Mask'. This mask represents people who are always boasting or showing off about their own lives, trying to make themselves sound better than they really are (like the way newspapers exaggerate things). This mask often fails because nobody likes a show-off. Very often people who wear this mask are trying to hide their own insecurities.

Explain that whereas the first three masks are images we like to portray to other people, we can also have wrong images of ourselves – the last two masks demonstrate these.

The toilet paper represents what many people feel about themselves; they feel a bit like the toilet paper – not worth much at all. Maybe, like the toilet paper, they feel as though they are just used by other people and then thrown away. If we aren't shown love by our family or friends, or if people have hurt us, this is how we can end up thinking of ourselves – that we're worthless. But that's not true.

The brown paper represents the way many people see themselves – plain and boring; they are no more special than anybody else, and not particularly interesting to be with. So that's why they cover themselves up by wearing one of the other masks.

Finish by asking them which mask they are wearing. Say that we don't need to wear any masks at all (take the brown paper layer off) – the Bible says that God knows all about us – he knows the real you underneath all the masks you might try to wear – and he loves us all with the greatest love possible, just the way we are. This doesn't mean that he loves everything we do, but he doesn't let the bad things we do, or the bad things other people do to us, stop him from loving us. Encourage them to love themselves, and find out more about God's love for them – the way we really experience this is by inviting him to get involved in our lives and becoming a Christian.